SUMMARY:

Switch

How To Change Things When Change Is Hard

ABBEY BEATHAN

Legal & Disclaimer

Table of Contents

The Book at a Glance

Change and success do not have a concrete plan; and neither do Chip and Dan Heath, authors of the book.

They only believe in the potential that lies within the cooperation between the rational, which they call the Rider, and the emotional mind, which they call the Elephant.

First, you had to understand the concept of change in order to move on to:

1.Directing the rider, setting a clear path for the rational mind and setting the starting point and finish line. Look for the bright spots and follow the light.

2. Motivating the elephant by appealing to emotions whether it may be positive or negative. At times, it is necessary to create problems in order to induce change, sometimes all we need is encouragement and a smile.

3.Shaping the path by removing the rocks on the road and filling the holes up just to make it a little smoother, and make the journey a little more bearable.

And then, it will be your turn to do the switch.

Through captivating narratives and underdog accounts, the book focuses on a pattern towards success as seen in everyday people who have accomplished great achievements through the cooperation of the rider and its elephant.

This book is about how people from all walks of life spurred change from few resources and little structural authority. One can only find the switch they seek through making these three happen: directing rider, motivating elephant, and shaping the path.

Witness how changing bowl sizes reduce popcorn consumption, how cooking sessions helped fight nationwide malnutrition, how a different therapy session reduced a parent's tendency for child abuse, how simply shifting a team's focus could generate millions in profits, how a game encouraged teens battling cancer to take their meds seriously, how powerful the mind is when it comes to believing in change, how firm employees turned into investors and changed their work industry, how wearing a vest decreased medication errors, how acting as a valor appeased children with bad behaviors—

And how a long, fulfilling journey ultimately starts with a single step.

Chapter 1

Three Surprises About Change

Change is a concept most people resist even though they encounter it for more than half their whole lives. From having babies, getting married, discovery of new technology to having smoking habits, and even being obese; change can be easy, and it can be difficult.

One reason why change is difficult is because the world doesn't always go your way. That's why the authors tried to present their ideas of starting change through one's own means.

These three surprises make a structural framework which is not a set path for change but only made for practicality and flexibility for various uses. These make no promises on making change easy, just easier.

This is the book for those who want to start change. To start doing so, it is important to clear of the misconception that change for every individual is different.

One Saturday in 2000, Brian Wansink who runs Food and Brand Lab at Cornell University and authored the book titled

Mindless Eating, conducted an experiment on irrational eating behavior.

Random sets of moviegoers were given buckets of popcorn in medium and large sizes. Within those is popcorn that was stale and is super low in quality since it was popped five days before.

After the study, the results showed that the bigger the container, the more people eat; their data showed that those with the bigger containers ate 53% more than those who had small ones.

Whether they changed the movie they played or the location of the study, the results were the same. The study showed how people ate for something other than for pleasure and finishing their portion.

The respondents, upon getting informed regarding the conducted experiment, refused to believe the results saying that their eating habits could not be easily influenced by something as absurd as the container sizes.

If you were handed the results without knowing the size of the buckets, your conclusion might be immediate: some people eat reasonably while others are big gluttons. Same as that with a public health expert, who would most likely suggest in finding a way to motivate the "gluttons" to find healthier eating habits by showing the health hazards of their current lifestyle.

So rather than forcibly changing habits and lifestyle, why not change the buckets instead of changing people's mindsets?

This is where the first surprise about change comes in: people problem is usually a situation problem.

Change has one thing in common; a pattern that can happen only if someone starts acting differently. First, one needs to change the situation not only by influencing the environment but the hearts and minds of those involved. But more often than not, the heart and mind disagree.

The human brain is divided into two: the emotional side which majors on feeling pain and pleasure, and rational side which mans the conscious and reflective parts.

According to psychologists and philosophers like Freud and Plato, between the rational and emotional, it is the rational side that must win over and the emotional side that must be managed.

However, as humans, our emotional side tends to win over the rational one--- making us a potential customer for the invention Clocky, a clock that runs around unless you chase it

3

around and turn it off. Upon its release, it immediately became a hit because instead of letting the user succumb to his desire to sleep, it allows the rational part of us to function.

But the point here is, if you really want to get up, you'll get up early with no drama or Clocky required, for that matter.

The authors described the emotional side as the one with strength, the Elephant. While the one holding the reins is the rational side which they call the Rider.

The Elephant and Rider are two peas in a pod. The emotional side is the counterpart to our rational for it is the one responsible for love, pride/self-worthiness, compassion, sympathy, and loyalty.

People need the elephant's energy and drive for change. It can only happen if you appeal to both the emotional and rational. With the rider for planning and direction and the elephant for gaining the drive or passion to do so.

But if you have the two at conflict, then there's a huge problem.

In a behavior study disguised as food perception or taste study, participants were told not to eat and were escorted to a room which smelled of cookies. Some were asked to eat the cookies while the others were offered radishes. Then came in a second group of researchers who required the participants to trace geometric shapes which were, in fact, impossible to trace.

The study's results show that the cookie eaters did not easily give up in solving the puzzle while those who ate radish did. As a conclusion, they found that people's self-control is an exhaustible resource, much like lifting weights which expends energy the more you lift.

Controlling and coping with emotions is taxing and shaves off one's self-control.

So why does this matter? To change is to change our regular behavior and to change regular behavior is to let the rider take control. Therefore, the bigger the change the more you need self-control and the rider, therefore it is easier to consume self-control fuel.

Another common misconception is that people can't change because they do not try to or is lazy enough not to. Actually, it is exactly the opposite. The second surprise about change is what looks like laziness is often exhaustion.

Jon Stegner, an employee at a huge manufacturer, believed that their company spent more than what it needed. In order to make this fact known, he showed his superiors a hundred sets of gloves to prove that they need to change their purchases to start cutting costs.

On normal cases, it would be easier to let the rider lead with analytical discussions and spreadsheet presentations to the bosses, but instead Jon appealed to his superiors' elephants.

Focusing on the riders will only give direction, but without the elephant there would be no motivation; without the rider there will be no direction and the elephant would be only go in circles, that's why the key to change is speaking to both.

Two researchers from West Virginia University aimed to encourage people on a healthier diet. They traced the problem back to milk and managed to campaign for low-fat/skim milk. They ran campaign ads for two weeks which showcased the benefits of low-fat/skim milk and showed that its nutrients are comparable to whole milk.

In addition, they also held a conference which proved to be successful in showing how much saturated fat is in whole milk which was comparable to five strips of bacon and one tube of plan unhealthy fat.

The consumers weren't ignoring the health benefits of low-fat milk. They were simply uninformed regarding its benefits.

6

This is the third surprise about change: what looks like resistance is often the lack of clarity.

That's why is it important to provide crystal clear direction by getting vague ideas out and start letting specific and clear ideas in.

One must direct rider, motivate elephant, and shape the path so change can be possible.

One good example is Donald Berwick's story. The mand and doctor who changed the face of healthcare by saving a lot of lives from the medical defects which affects an estimate of 10% in patient population.

First, he directed the rider and set a specific goal instead of a vague one: 100 000 must be saved on June 14, 2006—9 am. With a mere 75 employees, he did not lose hope for his endeavor. He proposed six interventions to battle the medical defects and made sure that these would be carried out despite the lack of manpower.

Second, he motivated the elephant by gaining the support from a parent whose child has been a victim of medical defect and persuaded hospitals to join his mission.

Lastly, he shaped the path through the existence of the one-page enrollment forms, clear instructions, and mentoring programs from other successful hospitals which later on persuaded more institutions to join his cause.

Despite the challenges, he managed to carry the change he had envisioned and saved lives in the process.

Direct The Rider

Chapter 2

Find the Bright Spots

In 1990, Jerry Sternin, who worked for an international organization called Save the Children, got assigned to help fight malnutrition in Vietnam by the national government.

Upon his arrival, he felt unwelcomed and was even pressured to show results by the end of six months.

From his analysis, he observed that malnutrition was caused by poverty, poor sanitation, lack of clean water, and ignorance-- facts which were what he called "true but useless" in relation to accomplishing his target within 6 months

So instead of fussing over the factors, he hunted down for the bright spots within the rural villages through the help from local mothers. Fortunately, he found them: the children who weren't victims of malnutrition despite being in the same circumstance as those who are malnourished. He thought, if other children can be healthy, why can't the others too?

Sternin wanted to show the mothers to direct their attention to what they could possibly do instead of focusing on the concept of malnutrition and the vague problems with no immediate solution like poverty.

He started studying what exactly was different with the healthy kids. He then found out that their meals were being distributed to four servings a day compared to two of others. Some mothers even actively feed their children instead of leaving them to their own devices. They also add uncommon ingredients to daily meals like some greens, tiny shrimps, and crabs that adds to their children's added nutrients, no matter how small of a contribution.

Knowledge does not change behavior. Instead of leading the mothers in a group talk on malnutrition, he instead arranged then into cooking groups where mothers' help each other learn how to properly cook and prepare healthy but convenient meals for their children. Every mother who had participated had the intention to save her child from malnutrition, thus the success of Sternin's appeal to their elephants.

It is important to localize the solution for problems within a community or a group. Bringing plans of change from the outside would only trigger the group's defense mechanism believing that they are in different situation, therefore they don't need the same solution.

By the end of his six-month deadline, Sternin had achieved his goal: 65 percent of the children became healthier. The change he started even continued to the next generations. Several villages in Vietnam adopted the system and soon successfully fended off malnutrition.

With little budget and no expertise, Sternin and his team were able to aid the malnutrition problem through faith in the power of the healthy children, their bright spots.

The Rider has a lot of strengths, but it has the tendency to overthink, focus on the negatives, and make matters worse.

This is a hindrance to change. Once the rider started thinking of his problems without direction, chances are there would be no solution anytime soon. It just plain analysis. That's why the bright spots are important because they serve as guiding lights for the riders. Once the rider spins it wheels with a direction in mind, change is bound to come.

John J. Murphy, the school psychologist, met the ninth grade Bobby who was referred to counseling due to bad behavior. After several conversations with Murphy, Bobby's offenses were 80% less than prior. So, what exactly changed Bobby?

Murphy is solution-focused in therapy. Unlike the traditional method which was archaeological in nature, he disregards history and focuses on the problem at hand. Solution-focused therapists like him use different techniques to discover potential solutions; one of which is when he asks the involved parties to specify signs of their "miracle" or simply their problem being solved. This line of questioning leads to the conclusion that they themselves could solve their problem. By asking the questions, and analyzing what happened during their miracle, the patient themselves suggest how they could arrive at a miracle.

Contrary to common belief that change is difficult, changes can also happen through little adjustments without much effort and hard work. If change is warranted, what you only need to do is recognize and understand your bright spots and work them out. It is only by focusing on what is workable instead of what isn't that change can be achieved.

However, this kind of mindset might be suitable for doing business.

In 2003, Richard Pacale, one of Sternin's collaborators, consulted for a company regarding its miracle drug for asthma that continued to underperform despite being proved to be effective.

Following the pattern of change, he did find the situation's bright spots: two saleswomen with a different kind of sales pitch. But instead of treating it as good news, managers of the company viewed it as suspicious and demanded the saleswomen to be investigated.

On the other hand, finding the bright spots for Murphy turned to be a good thing.

First, he helped Bobby identify the times when he was not getting into trouble and focused on it. It turns out, Bobby was much more obedient during Ms. Smith's class. He reasoned to Murphy that Ms. Smith was nicer, but he (Murph) didn't accept such a vague answer. He kept prodding until he gave specific signs of why he liked her.

He then advised the other teachers to do the same. Instead of prodding on Bobby's archaeology or approaching the problem with practicality, he found a bright spot and focused on it.

In the end, Bobby did not become a model student, but he definitely became a better one.

So, what's common with these situations? Both found bright spots, but each group reacted differently.

With Pacale's situation, it serves a proof that the rider's capacity for analysis is endless; positivity can be disguised as negativity in the eyes of those reined in by the rational mind.

According to psychologists, this phenomenon is caused by our partiality to negativity. People have been long focusing on negative emotions, turning down responses, bad character, and problems.

This is the main reason why the rider, who is spinning its wheels to generate a solution as big as the problem, alone can't bring about change; he is always out to look for problems which blinds him from seeing what could be workable at the moment.

Instead of being problem-focused, why not be solution-focused? Capitalize on our strengths and focus on the now. Small things spur big changes; even if those small things take months, years, or even decades.

Just like Sternin who was determined to explore a solution for malnutrition and Mr. Murph who was able to make things better for bobby, one must not wallow in the negatives but focus on the bright spots instead.

Even in failure, there is success.

Bright spots that can spark hope to make change possible.

Chapter 3

Script the Critical Moves

Donal Redelmeier, a physician, and psychologist Eldar Shafir, posed a situation dilemma about a 67-year-old arthritic patient to study how doctors make decisions. The doctor has to choose between surgery and the prescription of an untried medication for the patient.

A variation of this dilemma was that instead of one available medication to try, there are now two. Results show that from 47% of the doctors choosing the medication, after the option was increased to two, it decreased to 28%.

This is what they call decision paralysis. After having been offered a lot of choices, even good ones, it renders our rider unable to choose and is forced to revert to the original plan (which is surgery for the situation). Our rider gets exhausted due to increased number of choices which makes the decision human, but not rational—especially since the choices are good additions.

Recognizing this fact is important for we encounter excess choices all the time.

The authors mention three situational examples:

1. In jam free sampling, between having six and 24 jam choices, tasters were more likely to buy when they've only tasted six kinds.

2. In retirement, long-time office employees' participation in retirement plans decreases by 2% per the addition of 10 choices of plans offered; the employees were actually walking away from money they deserved based on their contribution to the company; and even

3. In speed-dating, young adults who meet eight persons in search of someone gets more matches compared to those who encountered 20.

Basically, decision paralysis ruins different kinds of decisions altogether and possibly job and life ones to. As we encounter more choices, instead of having more freedom, it holds us back from making decisions.

Also, it is not only limited to having more choices, but uncertainty plays a part as well. Change brings about more choices and uncertainty which leads the elephant to take the default path instead in return for familiarity and security. Even if the rider tries to direct the elephant towards change.

That's why for leaders or people who aim for real change,

17

focusing on the precise details instead of the bigger goal ahead is what they need. They need to set the starting point and start *showing* how instead of *telling* how it must be done. A successful change needs to shed off ambiguity and be started slowly by detail.

In 1995, Brazilian President Fernando Henrique Cardoso had approved the privatization of their country's railroads. The system was a mess and conflicts continue to pile atop the other. With so little funds there was so much to be done.

Alexandre Behring from GP Investimos Limited- a private firm which bid on the southern line- got assigned to managing the company's choice of tracks which was later renamed as Americana Latina Logistica (ALL).

With a mere 30 million reals, Behring understood that having the long-term fixes would cost them hundreds of millions which they could not afford at that moment. So he focused on quick-revenue strategies, opted for speed than top quality, and recycled instead of purchasing new parts.

Change is only possible if it starts with the little acts and decisions. But that's when it's the hardest because it's the details that usually need more work. Uncertainty not only tires the rider but pushes people towards choosing the "safer" default paths. In this case, clear guidance is needed.

The key is not just identifying every move that is needed to be accomplished but also focusing on doing the critical moves.

Just like what Behring did when he distributed ALL's attention and effort according to financial urgency. Their engineers repaired old locomotives, boosted its fuel capacity for longer running times, all the while garnering income and spending little through the help of recycling.

Three years later, from a loss of 80 million reals, ALL gained a net profit of 24 million. Behring's strategic decisions proved fruitful as he guided his people through hard decisions and eliminated uncertainty.

As shown by Behring with the locomotive systems and the West Virginians with their milk, change was possible by scripting steps towards achieving it. It is important to keep in mind that what seems like "obvious" steps towards change do not come naturally to mind. We need some pushing to do.

Campaigns that aim for change usually utilize vague informative delivery rather than specific goal-driven ones. Like the Food pyramid which only shows how food are sorted according to hierarchy but doesn't indicate how much should people eat, how often should people eat that kind of food, and so on.

What we need to do is translate the campaigns into actions. Instead of simply persuading people to be healthier, be more creative, or save more money; why not dive into specifics and start from there?

For switch to be possible, we must shift our focus from campaign ideas to specific actions. Be direct and spur movement.

But of course, this strategy has its limitations. Like Funderbunk's goal to change parents who are abusive to their children. The idea sounded a bit too naïve and idealistic even for their team, but still they worked towards its success.

With 110 abusive parent participants, half started anger-control management therapy (the usual treatment) and half started with parent-child interaction therapy that requires the parents to fully submit themselves to playtime with their children for at least 5 minutes a day.

It was first conducted in laboratory setting with a therapist coaching behind a one-way mirror. The situation proved to be stressful for the abusive parent because simply, their rider needed every action to be supervised.

The exercises continued regularly in order to develop instinctive behavior and reduce the effort by which the rider needed to manage their actions. Later, they were instructed to deliver commands with reason rather than arbitrary ones.

After three years of continuing the routine, the participants were evaluated. Those who undertook the anger control management showed 60% of reverted abuse behavior while only 20% for those under parent-child interaction

Yes, the problem wasn't completely eliminated but there is clear improvement just by changing strategies.

According to Funderback, the abusive and normal parents have the same goal but with different methods. It is the lack of understanding of their child's behavior that leads them to do what they do. Of course, this does not serve as an excuse but merely an observation at how specific strategic actions could aid in lack of clarity; which is often related to stubbornness or restriction.

The same year as the privatization of Brazil's railways is the realization of Howard, South Dakota's high school students of the change they needed to save their dying community with the help of their business teacher, Randy Parry.

The students made a preliminary research to find out what is the major cause of their decline. They found out that local people spent more money buying outside the county. They realized they need to start spending money locally.

Parry urged them to present their findings to the community. They prepared a presentation which was attended by eighty-five residents of the county, many of which are top figures of their community like the school boards, city councils, and count commissioners.

Their presentation presented a simple solution: spend 10% of their immediate income on their county and that would boost their local economy by 7 million. After a year, the result came out to be twice as their expected increase.

The rest of their newfound success came soon after as they started collecting more taxes, funding more projects, gathering support and donations, as well as founding 21st century business start-ups.

To the rider, big problems require big solutions. But the more complex the rider makes the solution to be, the less he gets things done. He needs direction instead of continuous analysis. Change is often resisted, but in the end, the key to breaking this norm is clarity; specific solutions for a big problem.

Chapter 4

Point to the Destination

In 2003, Crystal Jones joined Teach America and was assigned to Atlanta, Georgia to teach 1st grade kids

After her first evaluation, she knew it would take a lot of her effort and dedication to raise the kids to the academic level they were supposed to be in.

Contrary to another teacher who simply targeted to raise the average of the kids' aptitude, Jones presented the kids with a goal to look up to: moving up to be big, smart, cool third graders.

To further motivate her students, she started calling them scholars and encouraged them to share what they learn from school to home. By spring, 90% of the soon-to-be official 2nd graders has their comprehension level equal or above that of a 3rd graders'.

Change is much more attainable if we focus on what we can do at the moment; small but manageable actions that can be accomplished by the members. But it is also important to have a near-end vision; a motivational and inspirational goal we work towards to (just like the 3rd grader vision by Jones).

We already know the importance of finding the bright spots and instructing the rider. This time, it will be all about where we are headed.

Breast cancer patients undergo a series of processes before they are diagnosed, and even the treatment itself causes them enough stress.

As a surgeon, Laura Esserman wanted to change this stressful process where the patients undergo for breast cancer diagnosis and treatment. The root of the problem lies in the lack of coordination between the departments. As a mere associate professor, she lacked the resources to carry out her vision.

So she started small by operating a breast care center four hours for one day per week. As time passed, the service improved, more staff participated, and center hours were extended.

Later on, the Breast Care Center had its own floor in the University of California at San Francisco. Patients came in swarms and the center was recognized as a leading center for breast care.

She achieved the vision she had in mind.

That's the thing about setting a destination for your Rider. He gets to channel his strengths towards achieving the goal instead of just poking his head over and analyzing the facts.

It is also important that the destination be appealing to both the Rider and Elephant. Most goals concentrate on SMART - specific, measureable, actionable, relevant, timely- and often overlook its emotional impact.

The destination must both show the rider where to go and show the elephant why the journey is worth the effort.

However, a significant problem arises when the members of the team are not inspired. Action without commitment spells disaster in the long run. If the Elephant is pushed further from what it wants, rationalization takes place and the subject/s deviates from the set goal; with excuses ready at hand.

It also poses a problem in our personal lives as there are times that we ourselves have little hold on our self-control and breach the loopholes of our commitments with our own will. This is because we tend to lean towards uncertain commitments like "Be healthier" instead of setting concrete goals.

In order to successfully restrict or discipline ourselves, we must learn to get rid of the ambiguity and script specific critical actions instead.

Jim Vanderby, an oil explorer of British Petroleumin in the 1960s, managed to tap into multibillion reserves despite being discouraged to continue trying after several failed attempts. This proved to be a huge contribution to BP's market.

Years later, the reserves became scarce. Finding new ones needed a new set of strategies.

BP adapted and started focusing on finding bigger reserves instead of small ones and was soon hailed as the most effective oil exploration company.

But the costs started getting a little too pricey, and they decided to cut costs from 5 dollars to one dollar per barrel.

Drillers have been going from probabilities from probabilities ranging from 10 to 75%. Every hole has been drilled. But from the odds of the 10%, one 1 well out of 10 would be an oil reserve and that is not a good enough statistic. However, the rider rationalizes the drillers with the thinking that every probability is important and therefore we should drill.

To resolve this conflict, the sense of comfort from the statistical data must be eliminated and once again rein the rider in.

It wasn't until Ian Vann, BP's head of exploration at that time, announced that for the next drills, there should no dry holes, at all. Majority found his declaration preposterous but either way, this spurred them into much more careful action.

As the team went from explorers to geologists, they became more critical and systematic in evaluations to ensure oil reserve presence. Instead of succumbing to the whims of business partners to drill low-probability wells, the workers gained confidence to speak out and disregard the "strategic reasons".

By 2000, BP had tripled its success rate and improved far beyond their expectations.

However, it is important to note that black and white goals aren't always what are needed; just like with Jones and the aspiring third graders.

What's important is the cooperation between the vision for a pre-determined goal and the smaller actions directed towards it. It doesn't mean that you must plot the exact journey, because it is anything but possible.

Investors deal with a great amount of data and analysis before venturing. Investment and stock-picking requires work and research.

It is only by research that stock trends can be predicted that's why the presence of research analysts garner much attention and are ranked according to credibility through investor votes.

Shearson Lehman's research department ranked 15 in year 1986 and decided to hire a new leader, Jack Rivkin, with the goal of getting into the Top 5.

Upon Rivkins' evaluation, the team at that time was in its worst condition. To improve its status, he hired a partner, requested a bigger staff and more budget, got rid of unproductive members, and made changes in the compensation system.

He started influencing his team's daily work habits and enforced specific work targets within the group. He became the department's coach and boosted team mentality.

Within 18 months, their hard work paid off and Shearson analysts attracted more attention from customers.

In three years, Shearson climbed from 15th to 1st after having successfully predicting the up and rising blockbuster drug, Epogen, of the biotech industry. The success was thanks to the more than 100 analysts who worked diligently by calling several hospitals and pharmacies worldwide in order to estimate the drug's potential.

Despite the rider's weaknesses, he is a visionary and a tactician. He only needs to find positivity and direction. He needs to focus on the bright spots and be given a map with a starting and finishing point— the method for taping potential for change and planting the seeds of possibilities.

Motivate the Elephant

Chapter 5

Find the Feeling

Target, being the 63-billion-dollar giant it is at the present, started small like any other retail businesses like Walmart and Kmart. But with the help of several employees, it has risen to be the retail store it is now.

One of those employees is Robyn Waters who had worked for Jordan Marsh Department Store and had lived a life worth of envy; well, at least before she was laid off together with other workers. She never intended to work in Target, but eventually she did.

She worked as the store's ready-to-wear manager and slowly made her way into her co-workers' hearts and introduced her "trend-right" vision. It was the time when color-trend exploded in fashion shows and she decided that was the wave they needed to ride to be able to rise up the market ladder.

During meetings, Waters would place M&Ms on a bowl and see how people would react to colors. Then she began her mission of persuading her team members to trust the trend and get on with it.

In the end, her everyday demonstrations and showcase of color displays paid off.

Similarly, in a study by John Kotter and Dan Cohen, it was found that change lies by appealing both to thought and emotions, the elephant and the rider. It is achieved by making people see and understand why change is needed; the SEE-FEEL-CHANGE tactic, just like what Waters did.

However, making people understand can never be an easy task. Making the decision of whether to appeal to the rational or emotional mind gets confusing enough that even experts have a hard time getting a grasp of.

That's what Pam Omidyar, founder of HopeLab, targeted—make teenage kids affected with cancer understand the importance of taking their medication. Most teens do not adhere to 20% of their drug routines which is suspected to be because, simply, it is hard to follow. They decided then to look more closely into what drives the teens to skip their meds and later made a game, named Re-Mission, about cancer-fighting nanobots to help educate them regarding adherence to medication routines.

After the pre-testing, the game appealed to the teens on an emotional level and motivated most of them to follow their routines. According to research director, Steve Cole, it might just be because the game showed them they could be in control by taking their meds properly and not be the sick kid anymore. It was the gut-level emotional connection that had changed the kids' attitude towards their medication routines.

Most people who failed to make change possible often blame the lack of understanding.

However, it's usually because instead of appealing to the emotions, most appeal to the rational mind. And truth be told, we can't really trust our own thinking.

We tend to misinterpret and misevaluate ourselves much more than we do others. Most of the time, our elephant intrudes into our self-evaluation and leads us to having what we call positive illusion. We tend to see ourselves under a brighter light that's why we fail to orient ourselves and get lost finding our starting point and therefore not being able to see where we are exactly heading.

One way of breaking through the illusion was shown by Sitkin and Gail Anne Healy, Deputy Commissioners of Department of Youth Services in Massachusetts.

DYS had what they call Attila the Accountant; the authoritarian manager of their accounting department. He left no room for mistakes and everything has to be perfect. But his tenacious attitude toward his employees have been jeopardizing their checks' benefactors.

Several had tried to talk Attila to be more considerate, but their comments fell on deaf ears.

To make things better, Sitkin and Gail invited Attila over for a roadtrip around their benefactors' community. What he (Attila) saw were people barely making a living and getting through their lives; of course, no one had an office like his.

Form then on, even though he continued to be the authoritarian that he is, his reminders became benefactor-based. Instead of simply reminding about focusing on the accuracy of the reports, he reminds his team about working in order to deliver to the benefactors on time.

At times, it is necessary to create a crisis in order to induce motivation and at the same time, the needed change.

Professors, therapists, businessmen, and even health educators have started the use of this fear-inducing strategy to accomplish immediate specific goals. However, in solving huge problems such as global warming, it might get a little trickier.

Emotion is the greatest motivation for the elephant. May it be happiness, sadness, anger, pain, and even fear.

According to the psychologist Barbara Fredrickson, negative feelings have the ability to "narrow" while positive ones tend to "broaden".

For example, fear of what lies beyond the dark alley sharpens our focus and cancels any other thoughts that might seep in during panic time. On the other hand, a positive emotion like pride motivates us to pursue bigger goals, thus the act of broadening; from a small accomplished goal, to achieving a greater one.

Just like how Robyn Waters had instilled excitement in her co-workers through the approach of the subject regarding colors. She found the right feeling to nurture.

Big ambiguous problems don't need narrow-eyed solutions, it needs bright, creative, open minded thinking that is willing to find the right feeling.

Chapter 6

Shrink the Change

In a study of hotel maids and exercise, researchers Alia Crum and Ellen Langer discovered that those who were conscious that their maid work is exercise lost more weight than those who weren't.

For an estimated number of 10 hours a day, the usual hotel maid cleans at least 15 rooms. Their usual work exceeds even the average needed daily workout sessions. However, they fail to believe that their everyday work is indeed an intense form of exercise.

But the maids who were given the report had lost an average of 1.8 pounds four weeks after they had any clue about their everyday exercise. While the other group shows no sign of improvement despite doing the same work for the same period of time.

Another case that features how lowering the bar raises motivation is the stamp promo in a local car wash.

They gave away two sets of stamp cards; one has 8 blank slots the other has 10 slots with two pre-filled ones. Once the slots have all been stamped, the cardholder gets a free carwash.

A few months later, 34% of those with the pre-filled cards had completed their stamps, and availed a free car wash, compared to the 19% of the zero pre-filled slot stamp cardholders.

This kind of phenomenon may also be called the placebo effect, which has been long proven in the area of medicine. Both the informed maids and the pre-filled cardholders had shown more tenacity in achieving their goals than their counterparts. The sudden self-discovery or self-realization that the goal might be closer than they think boosted their mind-body cooperation which increased the rate by which they reached their goal or finish line.

Contrary to the business norm of raising the bar, lowering it might just be what the elephant needs in order to get more motivated to be part of the change.

That's what the elephant wants—a short road towards the finish line that guarantees immediate gratification.

And what if the elephant sees the long road instead? This is where the dread of starting or continuing the journey pokes it head.

Just like how it feels in cleaning the house, the more you put off working on it the more you don't want to do it anymore. It builds up the dread of cleaning the whole house until it no longer appeals to your elephant.

In Dave Ramsey's experience with debts, now a financial guru, it is of utmost important to keep the fire inside going. He says that the main reason why people with huge debts end up hopelessly buried in the red is because they fail to see how their situation improves even if they pay.

Contrary to what most financial advisers would say, Ramsey suggests paying off the smaller debts first before slowly moving to the bigger ones instead of paying the big guns first. With math, there is already an obvious choice; pay the one with the highest interest rate instead of focusing on the small ones.

However, Ramsey insists on his Debt Snowball Effect. He knows accurate math of the debts wouldn't keep those in the red going. It is the feeling of accomplishment and the act of moving forward that gives them the much-needed boost to continue working towards their goal.

The only way around this is to start things little by little without always thinking of the bigger picture. Start small and sooner or later you'll be surprised at the ease by which you continue to succeed due to the satisfaction you gain by finishing every single part of the job.

Shrink the change, start small, and let things flow their way.

Chapter 7

Grow Your People

During his college days, Paul Butler had been on the move to save a parrot native and unique to the Caribbean island of St. Lucian.

As a fresh graduate, he had been offered by the St. Lucian forestry department a job as their conservation adviser. It was an easy decision and soon, Butler had already thought of three suggestions for conservation.

However, the goals weren't exactly the short-term attainable ones. It needed resource and time; two things he and the department could not spare much of. So he set out to appeal to the citizens' emotional quarters.

He gave the bird the St. Lucian identity. He told the citizens that they were the kind of people who protected their own and the bird is one those.

He started campaigning for the bird by making t-shirts, songs, stickers, costumes, and even calling cards. It was through this kind of effort that encouraged the locals to finally embrace the bird which later on became part of their national identity.

Through the public support, the killings have stopped, and the species came back from the brink of extinction. But not only the bird became part of St. Lucia but Butler as well. He was awarded the medal of merit and was declared a full citizen of the country.

His efforts were further rewarded as his success became a model for a conservation organization called Rare which continued its conservation efforts and already held 120 campaigns that reached at least 50 countries.

Another related account is how Kathleen Davis, registered nurse and vice president of hospital operations, and Susan Wood, consultant on Appreciative Inquiry, managed to decrease the turnover of nurses in Lovelace Hospital Systems of New Mexico.

It started with them finding the bright spots and finding out that what made the nurses stay was their strong-founded identity and pride as a nurse. With that, they developed an orientation program aimed at encouraging nurses to love and dedicate themselves to what they do.

Change was realized once the turnover rate decreased and their nurses' satisfaction rate went up.

In the business world, a firm called Brasilata discovered the secret to their success by founding their own identity and turning it into their greatest source of ideas. Their work identity became their pride and strength.

Modeled after the Japan, the firm began accepting innovations from their employees and by 2008, more than a hundred thousand of ideas have already been sent in. Most of which they have utilized to improve product packaging and service. The addition of several new minds in their firm had been a crucial factor in their development and processing.

One way to motivate change is to shrink the change, and these situations show us another: motivating change by growing the people. And it can only be done by appealing to the people's sense of identity, reinforcing it, and continue lighting the fire inside them.

Shape the Path

Chapter 8

Tweak the Environment

People tend to overlook situational problems disguised as people problems. We are so quick with our judgement that it tends to bend the truth hidden behind the problem.

Similar to the situation with the study about moviegoers and eating habits, the business world had its share of situational problems. Just like the story told by Edward Deming about a fire incident in a flammable plant which was caused by machinery problem but the workers received the blame.

Most of the time, we are blinded by the gravity of the situations that we tend to overlook them as backgrounds for the people around us. We fail to understand that those situations have influenced the people we interact with, each and every single day of our lives.

Standford psychologist Lee Ross called this the Fundamental Attribution Error.

According to him, it is impossible to rid ourselves of this error. It is only by outside intervention that we can break out of its hold and pursue change. That's why it is important to help shape the path and make it easier for others to change.

A study by college students aimed to discover why some students donate and don't donate canned food to charity.

First, they sorted the students into charitable and non-charitable ones and proceeded to send them basic letter with simple information on the donation and where to send the goods. In the end, only 8% of the charitable ones donated and none of the jerks.

Then the surprise came with the second letter, with a more detailed instruction of the donation, what to bring, and where to go. Forty-two percent of the charitable ones donated and so did 25% of the non-charitable ones. Input of details made charity a little more bearable and raised the chances of student to donate!

At times, the situation only needs a little bit of tinkering to start change and influence others to do the same.

This also applies to our everyday life from or work place, traffic signs, ATM machines, and even grocery stores. Just like what Amazon does with their 1-click-ordering, they encourage people to buy from their site by making their process a little bit more accessible than most.

It also happened to a consultant name Peter Bregman, who

was hired to help a firm's employees to use an online time sheet tool instead of the paper ones.

The executives were ready to risk their employees' paychecks in order to get them to use the tool, but Bregman wanted to have a clear view of the problem first. Why do they not want to use the tool? Why paper?

The answer came expectedly. Doing paper time sheets were easier. The online time sheet tool had an annoying wizard companion who imposes his help on everyone at the firm. That was why several of them do not attempt to use the tool.

As soon as the wizard was cut out of the picture, the tool's employee use rose until everyone started using it.

Once Bregman changed the path, it changed the employees' behavior.

Just like how Becky Richards helped fellow nurses like herself shave off the lack of accuracy in giving out medications through the use of bright orange vests ordered online.

Due to the noise surrounding the place of medicine administration, nurses often get distracted which contributes to the decrease in medication assignment accuracy— which can be deadly in every way.

At first, the nurses were annoyed with the vest as well as the doctors. The nurses felt belittled with their supposed error-making capacity while the doctors hated that they could not call out to their nurses when they need to.

But in the end, the rates of medication error dropped 42% after the first trial and continued to drop as more nurses adopted the strategy.

Richards like Bregman cultivated the path and made change possible. This happened too to an airline groups IT group as they successfully finished repairs by having their own quiet time instead of being interrupted every minute in the cockpit.

Another way to shape the path is through self-manipulation.

Amanda Tucker, country manager for Nike in Vietnam, who by simply rearranging her furniture began interacting more with her staff. Rackspace whose employees soon were able to pick up calls from customers simply by eliminating the call queuing system. And even the books very own authors, Chip and Dan Heath who had tinkered with their laptop browsers in order to remove the distraction of e-mails, so they could focus in writing their book.

Self-manipulation is effective in a way that we discipline ourselves not by exhausting our riders but by simply influencing our environment with changes small enough to the naked eye but big enough to contribute to change.

We make bad behaviors impossible to do and make the new behaviors easier (to do).

Chapter 9

Build Habits

Mike Romano was a handyman who had quite a temper. At high school he threw a guy out the window and enlisted in the army to avoid the government. This he did successfully.

In the army, drug use was rampant, but he never involved himself in such. But a few months after, he was sent to Vietnam and got involved in a bomb attack and was sent to the hospital. There he tried his first opium. And again. And again. And tried other drugs, too.

The continued drug addiction among their military had concerned the American Government. It had no pattern, no specific class, race, or age.

Fortunately, after eight to twelve months, those who have returned home had slowly withdrawn from drug use and by the end of the year, only 1% of the veterans had been using drugs.

The change was attributed to their change of environment. They were in the war during drug abuse, when they returned the addiction failed to follow them home.

Habits are essentially tethered to our environment. It enables us to fly on autopilot mode.

According to a study by Peter Gollwitzer and Veronica Brandstarter, action trigger is quite effective in motivating a person to do a certain action. It sets a path for the doer to visualize himself in the situation and has more probability of accomplishing what he set out to do in the first place.

They said that the triggers divert your attention from distractions and encourages you to look at the pre-loaded task or action you have set before yourself.

A study on recoverees of a hip- or knee-replacement surgery showed that those who had planned where and how to spend their daily recovery exercise showed greater improvement through decreased recovery rates and less assistance needed during exercises.

Similarly, General William Pagonis also utilized the power of building habits within his troops. By simply requiring them to stand-up during meetings, his troops became more attentive, efficient and effective.

In a one-year diet study at Penn State University, the concept was also used to help dieters limit themselves eating after consuming two big bowls of soup every start of the day.

Instead of feeling hungry the rest of the day, they claim to feel full once the habit of soup-eating has been instilled in them.

Habit building also became handy to Natalie Elder, an elementary school principal in Tennessee, as she set out to correct raucous behavior of their school's kids. Every day the staff would greet the children with smiles followed by a general assembly the gym where kids were encouraged to show discipline. Every day was a cycle, and at the same time, an improvement.

Through the action triggers, an instant habit is created and now you have an autopilot system that does not run on the rider's self-control fuel. You get work done without exhausting the rider.

Change the environment and build the habit. Then watch the change happen.

Chapter 10

Rally the Herd

Change is uncertain.

During ambiguous situations, people tend to look to others for guidance. We look for clues and slowly figure out how to behave based on what we see. And that's one of the main problems about change; most of the time, change is our uncharted territories and we lack the ability to face it blindly, head-on.

This was demonstrated in a study by Bibb Latane and John Darley on Columbia University students. They observed how people as individuals and groups tend to react to emergency situations which present uncertainties. The results show that in both cases, only a handful acted according to their judgement or to the gravity of the situation. Most just stood idly by without doing anything,

Their conclusion? Behavior is contagious and most of the time, even unknowingly, people are more likely to do something because their peers do too. Your views of what is acceptable changes based on the views of the people around you. It has been shown in empirical accounts on obesity, drinking, fashion, and even marriage. When we don't have a clue how to act in a situation, we follow the herd.

That's why in promoting positive change, it is important to publicize when the herd commits to carrying out the right behaviors. This would then encourage the minority of the group to do the same.

But what if the norms turn against you?

In Gerard Cachon's story, he became editor of the operations journal Manufacturing and Service Operations Management (MSOM) in 2006. During his first term as editor, the processing of their journal's peer reviews takes seven months to one year. Compared to academic and scientific journals, their processing is already considered late. He thought the team needed a wake-up call to make their reviews get released faster.

So, he followed the pattern.

He spoke to his constituents and provided everyone with a vision—he decided they should get reviews out within 65 days. Next, he appealed to their identity as operations people as motivation. According to him, they should be the ones leading in terms of efficiency and time early.

Lastly, he set a specific course of action: every reviewer must be committed to review submission every five weeks.

Every week he posted every team members' progress and called out those who were not able to reach the deadline. This created work pressure and soon, as everyone started working much faster, their journal had the fastest turnaround time.

It is not only limited to peers: behavior is contagious even in society.

In 1980, Jay Winsten, a public professor at Harvard spurred a change in Americans' behavior which later on turned into a state-wide norm; the concept of designated driver, so that during drinking parties there would be one available person to do the driving.

He made it their team's mission to spread the behavior throughout America through peer exposure.

He collaborated with various TV producers, writers, and actors from over 160 televised shows in order to demonstrate stories that feature designated drivers.

Forward to year 1991, three years later, nine out of ten Americans have adapted the behavior and soon decreased alcohol-related traffic incidents. Simulating a social norm thorough the media proved successful.

54

Also, in 2007, a group of public health and AIDS experts utilized media to help aid the societal problem of Tanzania regarding cross-generational sex. During those times, sugar-daddies wee rampant and have been a major cause in spreading AIDS to younger generations especially to young women in their teens. This was a norm that seemed to be widely accepted, but in reality, silent protests all around were in motion; but never loud enough to fully counter the problem.

So, the group set-out to find a long-term solution and came up with a great idea; turning the concept of sugar-daddies into a laughable concept enough to convince people to shy away from people who are such. The idea was broadcasting a radio series in several radio stations all over the country that feature a sugar-daddy figure named Fataki.

Soon, the silent protests gained enough voice and confidence thanks to the efforts of incorporating humor into the sugar-daddy concept, rendering them powerless over holding authority over their victims.

Another account on proving how rallying the herd works wonders is how the introduction of a new identity language could aid in making change possible. In 1984, the death of an 18-year-old due to a medical error by an intern was a wake-up call to the society regarding the working hours of medicine interns.

Two decades later, after several legal processes, the American Congress approved the decrease of internship hours from 120 to 80. However, a study by the Journal of the American Medical Association showed that only 1 out of 3 programs applied the decrease in internship hours.

To understand why some have resisted the change in work hours, Katherine Kellogg, an ethnographer at MIT's Sloan School of Management, studied two northeastern teaching hospitals which she named Alpha and Beta. She found out that what contributed to the lack of the new program's effectivity was the failure of daily sign outs, persistence of residents, and work overload.

The sign outs were supposed to be transition between interns and residents every 9pm to 10 pm and most failed to do so and the interns usually work the whole day and the whole night too. In addition, they needed to finish readings and assigned tasks after their work hours or early in the morning before their shifts.

In Alpha, free-space meetings were conducted while Beta did not conduct any discussion of that kind. Free-space meetings were utilized by reformers to enforce change without supervision from the dominant members.

She set out to determine which of the two hospitals would better support the change in work hours after her study. The result was surprising; 66% of those from Beta proved to be more cooperative with implementing the change while only 42% form the Alpha.

The two scenarios in these hospitals proved that at times, individual character can go above situational forces.

Chapter 11

Keep the Switch Going

The journey starts with a single step but taking that single step doesn't guarantee finishing the journey.

Amy Sutherland, a writer who studied exotic animal trainers observed how teaching the animals takes hundreds of sessions and a lot of work and effort.

She tried the same concept, no matter how absurd it seemed, on her husband and produced an article on Times that gained a lot of attention. She penned a book about the same topic soon later.

Just like the trainers, she started little by little; through positive comments every time her husband slows down a mile while driving and tossing his laundry in the hamper. Soon, her husband, basking in her newfound appreciation, began to change.

This strategy is contrast to how most view improvement of relationships at work; which was that you identify the type of people you work with and you realign yourself with people whose attributes are most similar to yours.

According to the authors, this is an error in thinking of how to improve relationships since what we really need is to simply reinforce and acknowledge others' positive behaviors and hope they would do the same.

Reinforcement of these positive habits would be the key to get that one single step further ahead the journey.

The rider easily spots the problems and fusses over it, that's why in order to keep the steps coming we must reinforce and celebrate the positives in order to push the rider into the journey.

Change isn't an event; it's a process. Sometimes it may be easy, but most times it's hard.

It takes a lot of work and effort, but once it starts it continues to roll and build up; the snowballing effect.

At first, the change brought about by this will be unwelcome and unfamiliar, but as time passes it transforms into acceptance and maybe even adoration; mere exposure effect as psychologist would like to call it.

The best example would be the concept of being a parent and raising a child. It's a massive change and raising them works most of the time. Why? First and foremost, everyone became children and therefore they had the direction needed in terms

59

of growing up. This serves as a model for the rider; a guide. The change brought about by parenthood appeals to the elephant and soon grows into an unconditional feeling so powerful that you would be willing to do anything for your kids. At first, people around helps to your adjustment with change.

But when change works, it always has a pattern. Situations vary in scale, resources, intensity, and the people involved. But it always follows a pattern. As soon as there is direction, motivation, and a supportive environment; the rider, elephant, and path all line up—that's when change works. The key to succeeding, is to embrace this pattern instead of ignoring it.

Conclusion

Change is a concept most people resist even though they encounter it for more than half their whole lives. One reason why change is difficult is because the world doesn't always go your way. It is also a constant battle between the Rider (rational mind) and the Elephant (emotional mind).

In addition to the confusion, there are too many misconceptions about change, and here are some that might just surprise you.

In change, *people problem is usually a situation problem.* At times, we have to look beyond the people and see the surroundings. A lot of problems have been mistaken as human error, but in the end, the real perpetrators are outside factors.

In change, *what looks like laziness is often exhaustion.* People who have trouble changing are often mistaken as lazy ones, those who do not take the chance to embrace change, or even those who do not try. But in reality, it is the exact opposite. The process of changing itself as they will themselves against their rider is tiring. Self-control is exhaustible. Use it wisely.

In change, *what looks like resistance is often the lack of clarity.* Ignorance is what holds people back from venturing into the unknown. The fear far of the unknown that lies ahead stands in the way of renewal. It is only by making people understand and trying to understand themselves will make change possible.

Direct the rider by:

Finding the bright spots. The rider is well-known for his tendency to focus on the negatives. It is your task to find the bright spots and direct the attention of both the rider and the elephant to following the light and spreading it. Negativity is not unavoidable, but overthinking is.

Scripting the critical moves. Change is not possible with mere positivity alone. One must be willing to carry out the needed actions in order to pursue success. One must first identify what needs to be done, and sort things out according to priority. It is important to accomplish the critical moves, rather than mindlessly accomplishing tasks in order. That starts a greater kind of change.

Pointing to the destination. The rider needs a guide and map. It is only by giving the rational mind a view of the finish line that it stops going around in circles. With a goal in mind, the elephant is also bound to be moved along the way, therefore making change possible.

Motivate the elephant by:

Finding the feeling. Most people who failed to make change possible often blame the lack of understanding. However, it's usually because instead of appealing to the emotions, most appeal to the rational mind. And truth be told, we can't really trust our own thinking. At times, it is necessary to create a crisis in order to induce motivation and at the same time, the needed change for emotion is the greatest motivation for the elephant. May it be happiness, sadness, anger, pain, and even fear.

Big ambiguous problems don't need narrow-eyed solutions, it needs bright, creative, open minded thinking that is willing to find the right feeling.

Shrinking the change. Start doing things little by little without always thinking of the bigger picture. The satisfaction of achieving the small wins start a snowball effect and soon, you'll be surprised at the ease by which you continue to succeed after every step of the way. Shrink the change, start small, and let things flow their way.

Growing your people. The concept of change might break people apart but it is identity that brings them together. There are two ways to motivate change: shrink the change and growing the people. Appeal to the people's sense of identity, reinforce it, and continue lighting the fire inside them.

Shape the path by:

Tweaking the environment. To help others change, it is important to smoothen the path. AT times, it is not the people who are not motivated, it's just the road that is too bumpy. You could see how merely making the road flatter could motivate people to act towards change instead of against it.

Building habits. Habits are always connected to our environment. They allow ourselves to run on autopilot mode which in turn does not exhaust the rider. With habits, people can adapt to change through action triggers and slowly achieve their goals little by little, in regular intervals, repeatedly.

Rallying the herd. During uncertain times, people look to other for guidance. They say behavior is contagious, and so is change. Utilize the element of peers and its influence in order to direct the people into the change you want them to go into. It is only be demonstrating that you get people to do something.

Keeping the switch going. Follow the pattern and embrace it. Do not let yourself be afraid of change, welcome it and continue the journey one step at a time.

Now it's your pattern. What will you switch?

Final Thoughts

Hey! Did you enjoy this book? We sincerely hope you thoroughly enjoyed this short read and have gotten immensely valuable insights that will help you in any areas of your life.

Would it be too greedy if we ask for a review from you?

It takes 1 minute to leave 1 review to possibly influence 1 more person's decision to read just 1 book which may change their 1 life. Your 1 minute matters and we value it and thank you so much for giving us your 1 minute. If it sucks, just say it sucks. Period.

FREE BONUS

P.S. Is it okay if we overdeliver?

Here at Abbey Beathan Publishing, we believe in overdelivering way beyond our reader's expectations. Is it okay if we overdeliver?

Here's the deal, we're going to give you an extremely valuable cheatsheet of "Accelerated Learning". We've partnered up with Ikigai Publishing to present to you the exclusive bonus of "Accelerated Learning Cheatsheet"

What's the catch? We need to trust you... You see, we want to overdeliver and in order for us to do that, we've to trust our reader to keep this bonus a secret to themselves. Why? Because we don't want people to be getting our exclusive accelerated learning cheatsheet without even buying our books itself. Unethical, right?

Ok. Are you ready?

Simply Visit this link: http://bit.ly/acceleratedcheatsheet

We hope you'll enjoy our free bonuses as much as we've enjoyed preparing it for you!

Free Bonus #2: Free Book Preview of Summary:
Fat for Fuel

The Book at a Glance

The book focuses on the use of Mitochondrial Metabolic Therapy (MMT) to attain a healthy body. This particular technique aims to help in repairing and maintaining the proper functioning of the mitochondria. Mitochondrial dysfunction is seen as a cause of many diseases because of the release of reactive oxygen species (ROS) and the inability to promote apoptosis.

Research has revealed that high carb diets have a negative effect on this organelle, causing abnormalities in the various metabolic processes. Given that the modern American diet has become synonymous with highly processed carbohydrates, it isn't surprising at all that many end up experiencing mitochondrial aberrations. Thus, it's the aim of MMT to promote health by establishing guidelines and strategies that will ensure that the mitochondria stay in tiptop shape.

In the book's first part, the basic principles concerning the mitochondria, free radicals, and MMT are explained in detail. It also discusses the high fat, low carb diet that is recommended for MMT practitioners. Note that Part 1 is divided into five chapters. Chapter 1 focuses on the nature of the mitochondria as an organelle and its ability to produce free radicals. Chapter 2 deals with the reasons to undergo MMT. Chapter 3 talks about the use of protein and the dangers of having them in excess. Chapter 4 covers the use of iron in the body and its adverse effects (when present in great amounts). Chapter 5 deals with the diet involved in MMT.

Part 2 of the book explains the do's and don'ts of MMT. It's filled with guidelines and tips for a successful practice of MMT's principles. This part is divided into six chapters. Chapter 6 provides details on the preparation phase before undergoing MMT. Chapter 7 discusses the things that must be done upon starting MMT. Chapter 8 talks about transitioning from glucose to fat as the main source of energy for the body. Chapter 9 gives advice on how to stick with MMT for the long-term, while chapter 10 explains the importance of fasting and the proper ways to do it. Finally, Chapter 11 talks about other ways to help repair and maintain the mitochondria.

Each chapter of the book contains examples given by doctors. Actual health problems are tackled and readers are motivated by true success stories. Scientific evidence is used throughout the book, even those not directly related to the mitochondria but have an impact nonetheless. Without a doubt, the book finds ways to encourage the reader to adopt MMT for better health and a more fulfilling life.

Introduction

Joseph Mercola's early fitness lifestyle was highly influenced by his fondness of *Aerobics* — a book that, as some would say, eventually led him to go to medical school. Although he was technically involved in mainstream science (particularly in fitness and health), he was still intrigued by the most popular health fads of his time. He was particularly interested in the low-fat, high-carb diet that was actually doing more harm than good.

He eventually met Dr. Ron Rosedale and became interested in the critical need to control high insulin levels in order to prevent nearly every chronic degenerative disease. These diseases (which include diabetes, obesity, heart disease, cancer, arthritis, and neurodegenerative disorders) have become rampant these days. The author also read Travis Christofferson's *Tripping over the Truth: How the Metabolic Theory of Cancer Is Overturning One of Medicine's Most Entrenched Paradigms*. He then realized that chronic diseases and cancer emerge because of mitochondrial dysfunction, which actually creates limitations in the metabolic processes. Leptin and insulin receptors develop resistance because carbohydrates are taken in excessive amounts. Likewise, mammalian target of rapamycin (mTOR) signaling is activated because of too much protein intake. What happens when mTOR signaling occurs far too frequently? Tumors develop.

The mitochondrion is known as the powerhouse of the cell and its job is to convert nutrients (especially carbohydrates) coupled with oxygen into ATP or energy. This particular organelle can also cause living systems to function abnormally or not at all if it becomes dysfunctional. This is an important point of view when it comes to the study of cancer cells. Now, if a disease like cancer can start because of organelle dysfunction, then it can be stopped if that organelle is repaired. This is the objective of the author. He wants to educate the people in the possible techniques that can be done to help prevent and stop cancer and other related illnesses.

The author hypothesized that it all starts with the type of food eaten every day. A change in diet, from one that's loaded with carbohydrates into one that features high quality fats, will create massive changes to health and fitness.

To further learn about nutrition and its effects on the human body, the author met with Miriam Kalamian — a nutrition consultant, educator, and author. The two discussed the implementation of ketogenic therapies for people with cancer, putting emphasis on the importance of ketones in repairing the mitochondria and preventing cancer. Now, Miriam is the nutrition consultant for Dr. Thomas Seyfried, who is widely recognized as one of the leading pioneers in the metabolic theory of cancer.

All things considered, the author's goal is to provide a concise, clear, and scientific explanation about the effect of diet on the normal functioning of the mitochondria and the treatment of cancer cells. That's why *Fat for Fuel* gives a list of things to eat, convenient techniques to follow, and practical ways to track the things you're going to do in improving your mitochondrial health — collectively, this program is called Mitochondrial Metabolic Therapy (MMT). Again, MMT is composed of a diet regimen that changes the metabolism's reliance on sugar, shifting its attention towards the use of fat in producing the energy needed by the body. This shift will optimize the abilities of the mitochondria and will also protect the DNA from possible abnormalities.

The MMT diet is high in fat, moderate in protein, and low in carbohydrates. As you've probably noticed, this is considerably different from what is deemed normal by the American public. The usual American diet is composed of a lot of refined grains, processed sugar-loaded products, and low-quality fat. The MMT diet is actually more delicious and satisfying. It takes away hunger, cravings, and any feelings of deprivation. It also provides a noticeable energy boost. Aside from being beneficial to those already suffering from neurodegenerative disease (like Alzheimer's and dementia), cancer, type-2 diabetes, and obesity, MMT helps people who are looking to improve their overall health while slowing down the aging process.

The author puts emphasis on the number of studies showing the importance of mitochondrial health in metabolic health. At some point in the future, this different kind of therapy will be accepted as a standard for taking care of patients with cancer and most other chronic diseases.

Read More...